From H To Here

Turning Toward Enlightenment

Gary Crowley

From Here To Here: Turning Toward Enlightenment, 1st Edition

Copyright © 2006 by Gary Crowley
221 Witham Road, Encinitas, CA 92024
(760) 223-4279, Email: Crowley@pacbell.net
Website: www.garycrowley.com

Library of Congress Control Number: 2006928928

ISBN-10: 1-933983-01-9
ISBN-13: 978-1-933983-01-1

PUBLISHED BY GL DESIGN
2090 GRAPE AVE
BOULDER, CO 80304

Cover Photo by: Gilles Cohen

Table of Contents

A Note to the Reader

Dear Reader,

This "little book on enlightenment" is intentionally concise. Yet, many past readers have urged that I might encourage you to make sure and read the *entire* text. The slight sting of facing *what is* in the first half of the book lays the necessary foundation for the joy and freedom that is realized in the second half of the book--I wouldn't want you to miss out.

Yours,

Gary Crowley

Understanding What Is

Enlightenment is devastatingly simple. Although questions regarding enlightenment often become complicated, the answer always remains simple: awakening to enlightenment is the direct result of freedom from the illusion of a separate self. A profound understanding of this ultimate simplicity provides all that is required for an awakening to enlightenment.

Enlightenment is what we are. There is nothing to gain, only its recognition. Enlightenment's simplicity has been expressed in many ways:

I am, but there is no 'me.' Wei Wu Wei

You are the perceiving, not the perceiver. Ch'an

You are looking for what is looking. St. Francis of Assisi

That which is seeking, is the sought. Buddhic Scripture

The above quotations all express enlightenment's simplicity. The possible examples are endless; I just happen to like those that do it in seven words. As you will soon discover, understanding the essence of these statements is all that is required for the spiritual seeker because you are always already enlightened.

Your illusionary self is never the same once it is seen through. After decades of spiritual seeking, I read one footnote by Wei Wu Wei that changed everything:

Free, we are not the number One, the first of all our objects,

but *Zero* – their universal and Absolute Subject.[1]

This footnote caused a shift in orientation that cannot be shifted back. It was devastatingly simple and understanding was the only requirement.

Understanding is recognition, clear seeing. It is not the same as knowledge. In daily life, the words "understanding" and "knowledge" are often used interchangeably, but throughout this book "understanding" refers to a direct recognition of *what is*. We all can think of times when we had knowledge of something in our head, but it was not integrated, and therefore, was only a theoretical notion. As a child you may have been given knowledge that fire was hot, but until you ran your hand over a flame, no true understanding could exist. Now, whenever you see a fire, an understanding occurs, a direct recognition that fire is hot, without any need for abstract concepts about *what is.*

Without understanding, enlightenment's simplicity is missed. With understanding, enlightenment's simplicity cannot be ignored. The poet Rumi expressed this sentiment as:

I lived on the lip,

of insanity, wanting to know reasons,

knocking on a door. It opens.

I've been knocking from the inside! [2]

Awakening to enlightenment is a journey from here to here, not from here to there. There is nowhere to go and nothing to be attained. Enlightenment is simply an awakening to what has always been the case. There is only the seeing through of our own ignorance. The journey becomes a circle because it finishes where it started, but at the finish, one experiences the same world from an entirely different perspective. As a result, your case of mistaken identity effortlessly dissolves.

The release of an illusionary separate self occurs effortlessly through understanding what was never really there. The false self, though not ultimately real, is thereby devastated. In its wake remains only what we are, which is enlightenment.

What if awakening to enlightenment requires only understanding? What if this understanding causes the release of an illusionary self, something you never even were? Would you be willing to let go of something you never were if it allowed an awakening to enlightenment?

The masterpiece of enlightenment is already here. There is only the awakening to it. Innumerable masters have affirmed it is so. Upon awakening, one sage purportedly exclaimed, "Is that all *it* is?" He then laughed and went about his daily business.

Seeking enlightenment is like searching for a pair of glasses that are perched on top of your head. All efforts to find the glasses are seen as ridiculous once one understands the situation. How humorous it is to discover what was there all along!

What if the only complicated thing about enlightenment was noticing what had been there all along? How could one not be amused after all the searching? Perhaps, laughter will result when you realize that enlightenment has been "perched upon your head" all this time, patiently waiting to be discovered.

Look at the graphic of the black cube below. Can you see the black cube securely tucked into the corner?

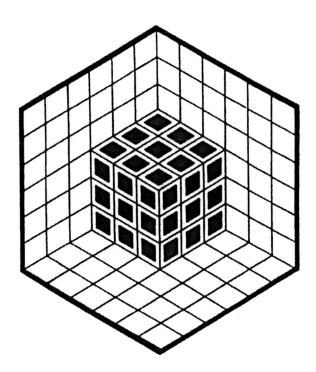

Now look at this same graphic, but see it as a large white cube with the front corner cut out. What was once a small black cube tucked into a corner is now a large white cube with the front corner missing. Notice too, that at any point in time you can see the image only one way. The image offers an either-or proposition in any given moment and cannot be both at the same time.

Awakening to enlightenment is like realizing you are not the little black cube tucked in the corner, but are instead the large white cube. Everything is completely different, yet everything is exactly as it was before. The difference is orientation. Understanding allows a different way of seeing what already is.

The required understanding is ultimately very simple, but unraveling your case of mistaken identity still requires precision. Human beings have an uncanny knack for self-deception when it comes to discovering their own essence. Ironically, spiritual seekers seem naturally conditioned to look in the direction opposite from where their awakening lies.

Like a child chasing the end of a rainbow, most spiritual seekers are forever *almost* there because they chase an illusion that will always remain just out of reach. With understanding, chasing the illusion ends as you realize that what you have been looking for is already right here, right now. This is why only a clear and unambiguous understanding of your illusion will steer you through self-deception and into an awakening to enlightenment.

Enlightenment may well be in an entirely different orientation from where you've been searching. All your efforts until now may have been like pulling on a door that needs only to be pushed for it to open. Once again, such situations are usually met with a chuckle when understanding finally occurs. Please remember this as you read the chapters that follow.

Enlightenment is readily available for those with the ability to face *what is*. This book attempts to clearly and concisely assist in this endeavor by wholly uprooting the cause of your suffering. Be forewarned: once the roots of suffering have been exposed, they are forever changed.

Suffering results from maintaining the most prized of all possessions, an illusionary self. The illusionary self is the ransom that must be paid by the spiritual seeker. When the arrow of understanding hits its mark, your illusionary self is its casualty. If this does not sound like an appealing proposition, then this book is not for you. However, if this description sounds intriguing, then let us begin the journey from "here to here."

The Science of What Is

Throughout history, science has assisted the earnest spiritual seeker in understanding more clearly the miracle we all experience each moment. While some may cringe at the notion of peering through the lens of science to enhance spirituality, only dogma suffers from this lens. Those seeking truth have nothing to fear. The following pages could potentially begin the process of a profound spiritual awakening.

Pre-Conscious Decisions

Our journey from here to here begins by examining how your neurology creates the linchpin of your mistaken identity, an illusionary conscious will.   Here and throughout this book, the word *neurology* refers to how your entire nervous system functions due to its structure and programming. *Conscious will* refers to your ability to consciously choose, of your own free-will and volition, *how* you are in regard to the world you encounter each day.

From a scientific perspective, it is your neurology that senses, interprets, and consciously perceives the world and makes the choices of how you will be in the world. The brain itself will be our primary focus because it serves as both the primary and final physical filter of your experiencing, and because without the brain there is no conscious awareness to be examined. As you will see, understanding how our neurology functions will make clear the direction our journey must take.

Most people would agree that you had no conscious choice in the DNA received from your parents at conception. Any reasonable scientist would also agree that this DNA provides the blueprint for your body's general physicality. Your eye color, skin pigmentation, potential height, predispositions for certain diseases, etc. are set in the DNA that is filed away in the nucleus of every cell in your body.

That same reasonable scientist would also agree that your DNA (which you had no conscious choice in) contains all of the intellectual, psychological, and emotional predispositions that will be expressed through your inherited neurology. The range and tendencies of all these attributes are hardwired into your genetic code.

Furthermore, you did not consciously choose the environment in which your neurology continuously developed as a child. The family and culture in which you were raised were very much inherited, just like your physicality. Thus, you had no conscious choice over the early environmental factors that molded and fine-tuned your rapidly developing neurology.

So far there is little to disagree about. We inherit certain individual tendencies, and our environment molds them. Francis Crick, the Nobel Prize recipient who discovered the DNA that makes up your unique genetic code, says it well:

> Suffice it to say that genes … appear to lay down the broad structure of the nervous system, but that experience is needed to tune up and refine the many details of its structure; this is often a continuing process throughout life.[3]

The environmental conditioning of your neurology occurs throughout life, but it is important to recognize that your conditioning began the moment your parents DNA united, creating your unique genetic blueprint. Your mother's biochemistry immediately affected your neurological development. If she was joyful or depressed, angry or anxious, her chemistry played a part in how your neurology developed, which affects how you experience the world to this very day.

For instance, suppose your mother was abnormally stressed during pregnancy. High levels of a certain stress hormone (norepinephrine) have been shown to permanently affect the embryo. Too much norepinephrine can make two deep structures of the brain (hippocampus and amygdala) oversensitive and hyperactive. These two *pre*-conscious parts of the brain decide when fear is an appropriate response. When they are overly active, your entire neurology will habitually react more fearfully to life than that of others. This type of neurology is constitutionally frightened. The pre-conscious structures of the brain are simply wired that way. There is no conscious choice involved at all.

The opposite can also occur. These two brain structures can be under-aroused in development, resulting in a constitutionally bored neurology that seeks continual stimulation. Conscious choice plays no part in these constitutional settings. Most of us have a neurology that is neither constitutionally frightened nor constitutionally bored, but rather, lies somewhere in the middle.[4] Of course, we also had no conscious choice in the matter.

To say you are not conscious of most of the brain's neurological activity is a profound understatement. Even your memory storage is *pre*-conscious. You do not consciously pick which memories get stored and which get ignored. It is the limbic system in your brain that determines which memories are important enough to be stored. Thus, the only "reality" a neurology remembers is a perception based on memories you had no conscious choice in retaining.

But it gets even better: Your interpretation of the present is also based on the memories stored in that neurological database you had no conscious choice in filling. Basically, the DNA that holds ancestral memories and reaction patterns, along with your personal memories, are the prism through which the world is interpreted. Whether that prism results in a perception of the world that is rose colored or some darker shade is not up to you, yet it is the prism through which your interpretation of reality is filtered.

Most lay people and scientists would agree that

neurological development as an embryo and a child involves no conscious choice, no conscious will. The question we must now face is the following: Is there any conscious will involved in the apparent choices made as an adult?

The rest of this chapter will show that your hard-wired genetic patterning and soft-wired environmental conditioning are not just the filters reality is perceived through; they are also the neurological dictators that order our reactions to any situation on a physical, mental, and emotional level. You have no conscious choice in how your neurology perceives a situation and no conscious choice in the reaction patterns it perceives as possible. The reaction to laugh or cry, feel frightened or safe, be angry or elated are pre-conscious reactions in the brain, based on memories that you have no conscious choice in prioritizing, arising from an inherited and conditioned neurology you had no conscious choice in building.

Howard Bloom's, *Global Brain*, provides a great illustration of the pre-conscious decision making process in the human brain. You can ignore the brain anatomy. Just enjoy the tour.

By now it should come as no surprise that said "mind" is actually a committee – let's imagine it as one which meets in a basement strategy room at the White House... The meeting is kicked off by the prefrontal cortex...which has been sizing up the situation for quite some time and now presents several strategies... The anterior cingulate... weighs the pro's and con's of the prefrontal cortex's game plans and passes a directive to...the motor strip – who shuffles through a sheaf of motor memories (that is, behavioral memes), holds a whispering session with – the superior parietal region – then quickly lays out a detailed action plan. At this point the president walks into the room, totally oblivious to the proceedings, takes the empty chair at the tables head, and is told the final conclusion. The president then strides out, holds a press conference, and takes full credit for deciding what to do...Consciousness and its theories are so far out of the loop that often we don't have the foggiest idea of what's going on...[5]

What you consider a "conscious choice" is determined by *pre*-conscious mechanisms in the brain. Thus, by definition, the choice is not conscious. Let's be honest: It would be a bit like the old Soviet leaders claiming they were elected by the people, when actually only one candidate was listed on the ballot and the people had no say in who it was. Just saying something exists, does not mean it actually exists.

Howard Bloom's analogy of the committee meeting is a wonderful prelude to understand the pre-conscious activities of the brain. However, we must also acknowledge the immensely complicated workings of the brain to fully grasp how "out of the loop" we, as conscious thinkers, are.

Any conscious awareness we have of the workings of our brains is not even the tip of the proverbial iceberg. Your brain has over 100 billion cells. Each cell links to 100 thousand other cells by way of synapses. These synapses constantly relay information. At a conservative estimate of 1 transaction per second, the brain computes one quadrillion operations per second. This is one thousand times faster than the fastest supercomputers, which means its capabilities far exceed any computer we can currently imagine.

Each moment of our awareness involves a massive "funneling" of neurological interpretations that end up getting filtered down and "tunneled" into our conscious experiencing.[6] Imagine many, many streams of neurological interpretations all winding together, or funneling, down into a finely filtered perception that we consciously experience. The interpretation of each moment is the result of a sorting through of all the opinions from countless committees. Each life situation is compared and contrasted with our ancestral and individual memories to decide what information is most relevant.

To give you a bit more perspective, take Howard Bloom's analogy (which is a great one!) of one committee and multiply it by 1000. Picture a round stadium filled with 1000 different committees trying to interpret a situation. Each committee communicates within itself and also has members running back and forth relaying information between committees. Some committees are specialized and some are generalized, some focus more on the past while others are concerned with the future, but they all funnel their interpretations to executive committee members, who filter it all and ask for more information from some groups and tell other groups they've heard enough for this split second, but to check back in one or two seconds with more information.

Some committees forward information about how the current situation relates to recent events. Other committees note how this situation is similar to other situations in the distant past. Still other committees focus on the consistency of the present interpretation as it relates to past interpretations. Consistency is a very high priority for your neurology. Certain data will even be ignored at times for that sense of consistency to be maintained. Lastly, decisions must be made so that the interpretation makes sense as a whole, so there is also a strong desire for completeness. The brain will even imagine things (i.e. make things up if need be) to create a sense of completeness.

Finally, the parts of the brain that are responsible for the final decisions filter this massive amount of "funneled" information and send it into the stadium "tunnel" for our conscious experiencing. These committees analyze and cross-reference each situation before presenting a scene to be consciously experienced.

Thus, your conscious experiencing is determined by an active, constructive, pre-conscious process and is not just a simple mirror perception of what is occurring. It is constructed by committees working in back rooms, hidden from sight. They are pre-conscious, and you have no say in the decision-making process. There is no conscious choice in the matter, no conscious will involved at all. *You experience what your brain decides you will experience, not necessarily what is actually happening.*

Your experience at all levels is due to the workings of your inherited neurology and its subsequent conditioning through the firing and wiring of neurons as you encountered life situations. Both function at a pre-conscious level and neither involves conscious choice of any kind.

Nature Conditioned by Nurture

The classic debate of whether nature or nurture makes us who we are misses the most obvious point: both nature and nurture shape our neurology, which shapes everything we experience. Geneticist Matt Ridley sums it up well:

> Inherited tendencies permeate everything we do, and they are flexible. There is no nature that exists devoid of nurture; there is no nurture that exists devoid of nature. To say otherwise is like saying that the area of a field is determined by its length and not it's width. Every behavior is the product of an instinct trained by experience.[7]

We all inherit massive amounts of genetic tendencies, which govern how we interpret and react to situations, which then govern how our neurology is conditioned, which further governs how we interpret and react to situations, over and over again. How we are as individual human beings comes down to our ancestrally based, inherited neurology being conditioned by the life we encounter. It is that neurology (which lies outside the grasp of any conscious will) that determines your individual experiences and reactions in life.

When considering human nature, I am often reminded of the classic scorpion and frog story:

> A scorpion needed to get to the other side of a pond, but could not swim. He spotted a bullfrog sitting on a lily pad and asked for a ride to the other side.
>
> "I'm not giving you a ride," the bullfrog said. "You'll sting me with your tail, and I'll die."
>
> But the scorpion convinced the bullfrog he would never do such a thing. He hopped on the frog's back, and off they went. Of course, halfway across the pond, the scorpion stung the bullfrog in the back.
>
> As the bullfrog was dying, he said, "Why would you sting me? Now we are both going to die!"
>
> The scorpion replied, "Because it's my nature."

It is futile to blame the scorpion for doing what it does. That's what its neurology does! That is *what is*. Denying the nature of *what is* does not change the nature of *what is*. Human beings also have a nature. Looked at from the proper orientation, it shows itself quite plainly. In *Candide*, Voltaire wrote,

"Do you believe," said Martin, "that hawks have always

been accustomed to eat pigeons when they came in their way?"

"Doubtless," said Candide.

"Well then," replied Martin, "if hawks have always had the same nature, why should you pretend that mankind change theirs?"[8]

Human neurology can and does certainly change with new conditioning. And our range of behavior patterns is much wider than the hawk mentioned above. However, the illusion of conscious will over such changes is just that—an illusion.

Each neurology's general nature as a human and as an individual is what it is, and each person's nature is truly not within the reach of any illusionary conscious will. In the chain of cause and effect, there will always be consequences for the way our neurology reacts. If your neurology takes you east, it gets the conditioning from going east, but will not get the experience and conditioning from going west. If going east becomes too boring or painful, then your neurology may seek out a different direction. Some consequences will fire and rewire enough neurology that it will shift your neurological tendencies; others consequences will not. That simply is *what is,* and it is not consciously up to any of us.

The Illusion of Choice:

Experiments In Social Science

It certainly does seem as if we make many conscious choices in life, *but there is a huge difference between choices we are conscious of and choices that are consciously made.* We may seem to have chosen to get an education, to not be a criminal, to not hurt others intentionally, and so on. However, upon investigation the appearance of such choices being consciously made falls apart as an actuality.

In the 1960s, psychologist Walter Mischel and two collaborators did what I call, "the famous marshmallow experiment."[9] It tested the impulse control of a group of four-year-old children. The scientist took each child to an observation room and handed the child a marshmallow. He then gave the child two choices: 1) The child could eat the marshmallow right away and not get another, or 2) The child could wait 15 minutes without eating the marshmallow and then receive an additional one. If the child could wait, he or she would then have two marshmallows. If the child could not wait, there would only be one.

About 1/3 of the children waited until the experimenter returned and received the extra marshmallow. Another 1/3 could not wait and ate the marshmallow right away. The last 1/3 held out for a little while, but not long enough to get the extra marshmallow.

These children went on with their lives and were revisited by the scientist 12-14 years later. He wanted to see if any differences arose between those with strong versus weak impulse control. The results showed that those with strong impulse control at 4 years old did far better psychologically, socially, and academically as young adults. The tendency was already there at the age of four. The supposed "choices" these children would make along the way were already very heavily influenced by their inherited and conditioned neurology up to that point in life.

The amount of impulse control a neurology possesses has real effects on the decisions it makes throughout life. All those decisions made to stay in school, not be a criminal, etc. were pre-consciously made by your inherited and conditioned neurology. Just because you were fortunate enough to inherit a decent neurology that was conditioned reasonably well by the environment does not mean you did it consciously.

Does your neurology make decisions? Yes, your neurology makes decisions. Does that mean you have true conscious choice? No, it does not. The decision-making structure of your neurology is pre-conscious. Reactions to situations occur, which we call decisions. But true conscious choice is not part of the process.

The billions of neurons in your brain have fired and wired themselves together in response to life in a way that makes your neurology truly one of a kind. Even identical twins with the same DNA will have absolutely unique neurological development. Our neurology ranks our values, needs, and wants for all levels of experiencing on our own individual scale according to our inherited neurological tendencies and how our neurology has developed throughout life.

You react according to how your neurology's pre-conscious perception of a situation meets the pre-conscious rankings of needs and wants for your completely unique neurology. If your neurology ranks "satisfaction in the moment" higher than "more satisfaction later on," your neurology goes for immediate satisfaction. It eats life's marshmallows. Period. All of these decisions happen outside of conscious awareness, even if you become conscious of them later on.

If a neurology receives more conditioning that changes its rankings, then the neurology reacts differently. If being a bully ranks higher than being nice, then the neurology reacts like a bully. When the bully gets punched in the nose, the rankings may change. It's all genetics and conditioning, cause and effect. It's nature and nurture, and there is no conscious control. Just because a neurology gets punched in the nose and changes does not mean there was a conscious choice to change, even if they eventually became conscious of the decision to change.

In the 1960s Stanley Milgram did a now-famous experiment that vividly reflects the neurological tyranny we live under. He took 40 normal people and told them they were part of a study on how "negative reinforcement" affects learning. In fact, it was all a set-up. The scientists were studying how the 40 volunteers would respond to a perceived authority.

The 40 people were required to electrically shock a student

(an actor who was not really being shocked) when questions were answered incorrectly. The person doing the shocking and the student were in adjoining rooms. They could hear each other through an intercom, but there was no visual contact between them.

During the experiment, the voltage of each shock was increased with every wrong answer. With each increase in voltage came increased cries of severe pain, heart problems, and agonizing pleas to stop the experiment by the one being shocked (the actor). Yet, not a single person stopped shocking the student with these initial signs of distress.

> … not one of the forty subjects in this study quit his job as Teacher when the victim first began to demand his release; nor later, when he began to beg for it; nor even later, when his reaction to each shock had become, in Milgram's words, "definitely an agonized scream."[10]

Every one of the 40 subjects knowingly shocked the student all the way up to 300 volts. Ouch! Your outlet at home is only 110 volts, and that hurts a lot! Two-thirds of people kept right on shocking the victim all the way up to 450 volts as long as the perceived authority (some guy in a white lab coat) encouraged them to continue. Fortunately, the shocking of the people was all faked. However, these "normal" people doing the shocking did not know this. Many of the subjects agonized over pulling the lever as the voltage increased; yet, they still did it. All they knew was that someone they perceived as an authority was telling them to continue.

All of us like to think we would act differently. Relate this study to virtually anyone, and without fail they feel they would somehow be the exception. The truth is that the odds are against us. This experiment has been repeated in Australia, Italy, Spain, Germany, Holland, and Jordan with the same results.[11] There is a pre-conscious neurological response when we are in the presence of a perceived authority over which there is no conscious control.

If you think about it for a moment, it's not so mysterious. We were all raised as children with parents and teachers whose authority helped us navigate the world; ignoring their dictates often led to negative consequences. We bow to authorities called doctors, policemen, and accountants all the time when it comes to physical and mental health, personal safety, and the IRS respectively. It's quite frequently a beneficial thing to do, so our neurology often makes the pre-conscious decision to lead us down the path of acquiescence, even when it might not serve us.

Thirty-nine professional psychiatrists and psychologists were asked to predict the results before this shocking experiment was performed. They all grossly underestimated the percentage of people who would continue the shocking despite the cries of the person being shocked. These professionals felt only an abnormal person would continue the shocking. They could not have been more wrong. Your pre-conscious neurological functioning determines your reaction patterns. The illusion of conscious will runs deep, but it is still an illusion.

Another famous study sent its subjects in opposite directions by putting the subjects in an environment that they were fully aware was fake. A Stanford University Professor, Phil Zimbardo, enrolled normal, well-adjusted college students in a mock prison experiment. It all seemed harmless enough, but the results deserve our attention. Professor Zimbardo's website states the following:

What happens when you put good people in an evil place? Does humanity win over evil, or does evil triumph? These are some of the questions we posed in this dramatic simulation of prison life conducted in the summer of 1971 at Stanford University.

How we went about testing these questions and what we found may astound you. Our planned two-week investigation into the psychology of prison life had to be ended prematurely after only six days because of what the situation was doing to the college students who participated. In only a few days, our guards became sadistic and our prisoners became depressed and showed signs of extreme stress.[12]

The experiment had to be stopped half-way through because the guards were abusing the prisoners (their classmates!). The (pretend) prisoners were stressed enough to begin conspiring against the guards. The environment very quickly took on the qualities of a real prison. The environment triggered reactions that are pre-programmed into our neurology. Apparently, their conscious will was out of town for spring break.

One of the students in the Zimbardo experiment jokingly wore mirrored sunglasses like those worn by a vicious prison guard in the movie, *Cool Hand Luke*. The student later stated that he was surprised and ashamed how much he became like the guard in the movie. Once his pre-conscious neurology had made the decision, he had very little conscious choice in the matter.

The concept of conscious will ignores the neurological tyranny under which bodies live. No medical professional or layperson in the Milgram or the Zimbardo experiments predicted how pre-programmed our neurology is. For a spiritual seeker, the importance of this understanding cannot be underestimated.

If, despite the evidence, you do not believe our inherited and conditioned neurology determines our interpretations and reactions to situations, then I seriously ask you to consider what does determine it. Is it divine intervention? Is it something else that we are not conscious of? Please note that neither of these alternatives brings conscious will back into the equation. Sorry to be a stickler, but if we are not conscious of it, then it cannot be conscious will.

The understanding you have just been given of your neurological functions has shown that your experience of conscious will is, in actuality, an illusion. The next chapter explores how the illusion works.

Illusions of What Is

If conscious will is an illusion, as claimed, then it is important to understand *how* illusions work. As the human brain goes about interpreting the world, it operates primarily as a pattern-seeking machine. For both survival purposes and practicality, it naturally seeks continuity. Imagine for a moment what it would be like if your brain did not do this. Every situation you encountered each day would be a brand new experience in every way. Just think how long it would take to get ready in the morning!

The sense of continuity is such a high priority that our brain will often do what the average person would find hard to believe: it makes things up. Our brains frequently form concepts and see patterns that are totally illusionary. The human brain prioritizes consistency and completeness over accuracy in order to maintain an illusionary continuity.

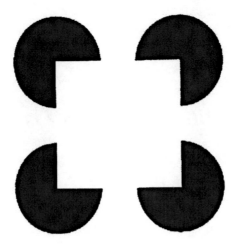

The image above is called a Kanizsa Square. It is a good example of your mind seeing a pattern that is not really there. There are really only four black pacman shapes, but your mind imagines a square. The square even appears more luminous than the same shade of paper around it. The square is "not really there," as they say. If you cover one or two of the pacmen with your thumb, the illusion of the square disappears.

Throughout life, your nervous system senses data, but your brain makes the pre-conscious decisions determining what will actually be experienced or perceived. It is the same with your illusion of conscious will. Your neurology has decided to interpret the experiencing of the world in a certain way, but much of it is "not really there."

The variety of images like the Kanizsa Square is endless. Your neurology is capable of imagining many things that are not really there. Look at each of these shapes below for a moment and notice the illusions your neurology creates. Then cover a segment or two of the image with your finger and notice what happens to the illusion.

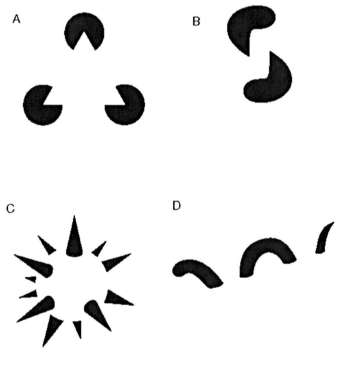

A: the Kanizsa triangle   B: Tse's volumetric worm

C: Idesawa's spiky sphere   D: Tse's "sea monster"

Conscious will is just another imaginary pattern that gives the body a sense of continuity, when in actuality, it's not really there. It is a way for your brain to make sense of experiencing the world through time. This way of experiencing the world is typical of most human neurologies. Seeing conscious will for what it is, an illusion, is the first step toward living as you truly are. As the glue of the illusion is dissolved, your case of mistaken identity can be naturally resolved. For the spiritual seeker, seeing through the illusion of conscious will is the fulcrum of awakening.

Pay attention to what happens as you look at the image below.

Most neurologies will see concentric circles coming out from the center of the image. They will also see white dots at the intersections of the lines. The illusionary concentric circles and white dots are just an example of what is called "good continuation." Your brain tries to make sense of the information by tying all the points together. It does so by imagining things that are not there.

The graphic above has too many separate points of intersection for your neurology to process. It makes more sense to imagine circles and dots over the actual design. The separate points of intersection can be *connected by the illusion* to make the actual design more palatable. All those imaginary lines and dots are like your illusionary conscious will. They are not really there, even though you experience them.

The actions of all human bodies are really just neurological reactions to situations. If the black lines are like the situations your neurology has encountered, then the intersections are where your neurology reacted with a thought, feeling, or action. The imaginary concentric circles are like the story you imagine about all the conscious choice you had regarding the situation. The imaginary dots are like the illusionary "conscious choice" you made.

You can see and sense the white circles and dots. But when you pay close attention, you understand they are an illusion. Those concentric circles and dots are just like the conscious will you move through life with. They only seem real.

Conscious will is not really there, yet we experience it. Quite simply, conscious will is a phantasmagorical imagining! The neurology that was inherited and was fine-tuned according to life experiences pre-consciously manufactures your thoughts, feelings, and actions. No conscious choice occurs anywhere in the process. Please read this paragraph again!

Your conscious will is an imaginary steering wheel placed in front of you on the train ride called life. You may be under the illusion that you can steer in any direction you like, but your neurological tracks determine where the train goes.

Look at this next picture for a few seconds. Really look at it.

This static image seems very active to your neurology. It pulses and shimmers. It looks like a three-dimensional sphere, and if you look at it long enough, petals on a flower appear and continue to change.

The illusions that occur when viewing this static image are examples of what is called "optical distortion." The neurology that interprets your visual data is especially sensitive to edges, but there are too many black and white edges for your neurology to deal with. In your neurology's continual quest for continuity, it deals with the overwhelming amount of data by creating the illusions of movement, three-dimensionality, and flow, but it's really a neurological misinterpretation.

Perceiving yourself as an entity moving through life with a constantly flowing conscious will is also a neurological misinterpretation in name of continuity. If you had to deal, on a conscious level, with all the "edges" of cause and effect for every situation in your life, it would be overwhelming. Your pre-conscious neurology does its best to pick out the pieces that give you a sense of continuity and ignores the rest. The illusion of conscious will is merely an overall sense of continuity that our neurology creates.

It's much like the blind spot in your field of vision caused by the presence of your optic nerve. Where the nerve attaches to your retina, there are no photoreceptors, so your neurology takes a guess and fills in the blank area as best it can. You never notice the ever-present blind spot because it's covered by an illusion. So too, your illusionary sense of conscious will is just an illusionary filler for all the pre-conscious decision-making processes of your neurology.

Look at the above images again. The illusion does not disappear just because there is an understanding of it. In the movie, *The Wizard of Oz*, the curtain is pulled aside to reveal an ordinary man working a machine that is projecting the image of a wizard. Dorothy can see both the illusion and the reality, but the illusion does not have any power to fool her anymore. Everything changes once you look behind the curtain, even when everything appears the same.

The illusion of conscious will is very strong. Many spiritual seekers have such contempt for the concepts presented here that it prevents authentic investigation. In the end, all the awakened can do is point out the illusion of conscious will for those inclined to look. Keep in mind that the investigation is worth it. Only when you discover *what is*, are you able to reside in *what is*.

Mental and Emotional Reflexes

Just as our bodies have physical reflexes, our minds have mental and emotional reflexes. The only difference is that with mental and emotional reflexes, there is an illusion of consciously choosing them.

There is a carnival game from the Old West you are

welcome to try. First, find a large jar made from very thick glass. Second, place a large, angry rattlesnake in the jar. Third, place your hand firmly against the outside of the jar and stare at the rattlesnake. Fourth, keep your hand pressed against the jar as the rattlesnake strikes.

For those who may not have a rattlesnake handy, I'll tell you what happens: everyone pulls their hand away as the rattlesnake strikes. In the Old West, one cowboy after the next would watch his friends bet their money and fail. Then he would try and fail as well. It's a physical human reflex to pull your hand away from the jar. The body just reacts. No choice is involved.

The carnival worker understood that the reaction of the cowboys was not a matter of conscious will. When it comes to a physical reflex, most of us would concede that no true "choice" or conscious will is involved. The reaction pattern is deeply embedded within us, so when we encounter a situation, our bodies just follow the program.

The illusion of conscious will simply masks the fact that our mental and emotional 'choices' are neurological reflexes, just like our physical reflexes. They are just more idiosyncratic. The cowboys who decided to gamble away their hard-earned money did not really choose to do so in the way most people think. Their mental and emotional neurological patterns were just walking through the carnival as they ran into a man who offered them a chance to win some easy money. Some took the bet; others did not. It all depended on the thoughts and feelings that arose upon encountering the carnival worker, which were pre-consciously decided. The situation then played itself out according to each cowboy's inherited and conditioned neurology.

Now here's the fun part: Our neurology can change if there is new conditioning. Your neurology is part of the chain of cause and effect like everything else. Many cowboys who lost their money the first time would not take the bet a second time. This is new conditioning. Yet, other cowboys had their neurology wired in such a way that a change did not occur, and they kept betting until all their money was gone. Either way, they may become conscious of their choices, but they were not choices that were consciously made.

The Loopy Nature of Our Neurology

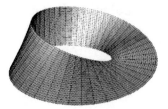

If human beings had conscious will, they would be capable of going against their own neurology. Yet, our neurology is all we have to interpret and react to a situation. The functioning of your neurology is like riding on the "mobius loop" pictured above, which can only continually wind back into itself. Your neurology constantly interprets and reacts to situations through the prism of its past inheritance and conditioning; the consequences of those interpretations then become more interpretations for your neurology to shape and be conditioned by. There is no way to get ahead of, or outside of, the loop, so there is no place for conscious will to exist. You are forever looking at the present through a lens of your neurological past because it's the only tool you have.

Our illusion of conscious will is supported during those times when we appeared to choose what was already manifesting in the chain of cause and effect. The neurological pattern-seeking machine we call a brain ignores the times when what we choose does not manifest, so the illusion of conscious will continues. "Continuity at all costs," is the daily mantra of your neurology.

At this point, some of you may attempt to go deeper into your human physiology to uncover this phantom called conscious will. You may be intrigued by the anterior cingulate, basal ganglia interactions, or other deep-seated anatomical elements. However, the deeper you go into your physiology, the more unconscious the mechanisms of your reactions become. For example, how conscious are you of your pituitary gland? You are not conscious of it at all. That is the entire point. For those of you still hoping to salvage your illusionary conscious will, I ask you to again consider, if its not our neurology that is doing the interpreting and reacting, what else is there?

The Sufi mystic Gurdjieff said people are simply "bags of chemicals." Nobel Laureate Francis Crick said "you're nothing but a pack of neurons." [13] People are walking, talking neurologies. Period. In the perpetual chain of cause and effect, which is our world, you do not get to consciously choose the links in your chain, nor does anyone else. Like spokes appearing to move backward on a forward spinning wheel, conscious will is an illusion your neurology creates to make sense of its experiencing of life.

Your neurology exists in the tide of destiny and is tossed by the waves of circumstance. A separate individual with conscious will is the illusion I refer to as the "me," and the "me" is what most people consider themselves to be. There is no conscious will, so there is no "me." The "me" is a myth, an imagining. When you identify so strongly with an illusionary "me," there can be no awakening to enlightenment. You have been pounding on a wall that is not even there.

The Illusion of Conscious Will

Once it can be clearly seen that the technique of "me," the habit of viewing the world from a position of an independent entity with conscious will, is a case of mistaken identity, then all the hard work is done. This chapter aims toward a final "seeing through" of the illusion of conscious will, so you will be free to embrace the eternality of what you are in the chapters that follow.

Let's take a look at an often unexamined assumption that the illusionary "me" carries with it everywhere. It's the illusion that "I and others can control what we think." It's very simple to see past, yet people use it to interpret their daily human interactions all the time. For example, try the following experiment:

Pick a topic you would like to think about for 10 minutes. Your goal is to think about only that topic for ten minutes.

Now grab a paper and pen and write down every thought you have for the next ten minutes. Notice how many thoughts pop into your head that are not about your topic. There will be a lot.

Oh—and this is very important—whatever you do, do not think of a pink hippopotamus while you do this exercise. Oops!

After the exercise, answer this question: If I cannot control my own thoughts, why would I think other people can?

Thoughts and feelings are no different than other processes of the body. The circulation of blood, cell replication, digestion, and so on, all occur without us consciously controlling them. We may become conscious of our thoughts and feelings, but we still do not control them. Although this may be shocking, it simply is *what is*.

Has your neurology ever been in love with someone and not wanted to? Or has your neurology ever disliked someone and not wanted to? Wouldn't everyone simply choose to enjoy the job they go to each day if they had the conscious choice to do so? If conscious will was more than an illusion, wouldn't both your physical body and psyche be better served? Seriously, wouldn't a lot of things in your life be very different if conscious will actually did exist?

Is it really valid to believe that people consciously choose to be the way they are? If an addict, a depressed person, or even a continually remorseful abuser could actually choose to become more functional, don't you think they would? Do you think they consciously choose to be unhappy and ruin their lives? Even the ones who have actively sought help? Seriously, if conscious will exists, who would consciously and willfully choose to ruin their lives when they could simply stop what was causing harm and do whatever was required to make their lives better?

Some of you will answer the questions above by saying, "OK, fine. If you are going to be a stickler ... I guess they do not *consciously* choose to be miserable." That leaves only the pre-conscious mechanisms of the brain doing the deciding!

Many spiritual seekers valiantly attempt to salvage their fading conscious will by introducing some version of the grand exception such as, "but what about the poor, inner-city kid who decides he's going to create a better life and does so? Isn't he an example of conscious will at work?"

The grand exception only proves the point that it's not about conscious will. I will often reply with another question, "What about the hundreds of other children that do not get out of the inner city? If they had conscious will, wouldn't they choose to have a better life as well? Or even better, "What about all those children who also *chose* to get out and didn't make it? What about their conscious will? They made a choice, and it didn't work out."

The notion of competing conscious wills pokes even more holes in the illusion. How much conscious will is there if your conscious will can be canceled by someone else's conscious will? If you have ever experienced being mugged, violated, or had a loved one leave when you did not want them to, you can sense that we really do not have control. How does it work for this illusionary conscious will when someone else's conscious will runs over yours? It usually leads to a great deal of suffering because your entire identity is based on this one illusion.

However, keep in mind that this question about the clash of separate conscious wills is like asking who would win a fight between The Incredible Hulk and Spiderman. Neither superhero exists! This, again, is the whole point.

The Shell Game

A separate "me" chasing enlightenment is the classic "shell game" of spiritual seeking. As the magician moves the three shells round and round, he hides the ball between his fingers. No matter how earnest your search, the illusionary ball never appears under the shell you choose, because it's not really there to be found! If you buy into the illusion, you are forever tricked. A "me" with its illusion of conscious will can never win at the "shell game" of enlightenment.

There is no "me" with conscious will that does anything! Human beings are nothing more than puppets whose strings are made invisible by the illusion of conscious will. Pretending the strings are not there causes suffering. Seeing the neurological strings begins the turning of awareness toward an awakening to enlightenment.

Jolly Charlie's Amusement Park, or "Jaalee Chaalee's" as neurologies from Rhode Island pronounce it, had a great ride when I was a little boy. It consisted of a series of little boats attached to a track that ran beneath the water. Although the path of the boats was predetermined, we were all completely fixated on steering our boats. We madly turned the steering wheel to avoid crashing into the stationary buoys that appeared in our path and were so pleased with ourselves as we barely escaped disaster. We had a fantastic time waving to the parents each time we would pass. What could be more fun at that age than captaining a boat?

Of course, for the adults, the boat ride was a completely different experience. The adults understood that the steering of the boats was all an illusion. They could not step back into the dream of a small child. Seeing through the dream forever changes the dream. Yet, the adults did not go out of their way to ruin the illusion for their children. There came a time in the natural course of events when the child had enough life experience to understand the illusion. With understanding, the child became an adult.

Similarly, the "ride" of a body with conscious will is nothing more than an illusion, a childlike fantasy. Once this understanding occurs, everything is different. Yet, everything also remains the same. The body is still on this ride of life, but with no ability to consciously steer the boat, we are left as the awareness of the ride. We are left totally free to be the experiencing of each moment.

Conscious will is nothing but a false rumor. This false rumor, this nonexistent phantom, has been causing all your suffering. The illusion of conscious will is the culprit that holds back your spiritual awakening, but like all illusions, it is only supported by a lack of investigation and a desire to believe what is false. Believing in conscious will is like a child who imagines there is a monster in the closet. The child is genuinely frightened, but a simple investigation quickly resolves the problem. Adults just open the closet door and look.

As a spiritual seeker, it is your nature to be curious about *what is*. This is not the case with everyone. Most human beings are fully immersed in the illusion and do not yearn to understand it. Your curiosity has brought you to a precipice. There is now only one question: Is there a desire to look over the edge?

"Come to the edge," he said.

"But Master, there is much we still do not know."

"Come to the edge," he said.

"But Master, we require more practice."

"Come to the edge," he said as he pointed, "And just look."

They looked… They understood…They flew.

By investigating the illusion of conscious will, the following becomes clear:

- No conscious will was involved in choosing the body's inherited neurology. No conscious will was involved in how that inherited neurology fired and wired itself together as it encountered life situations.

- Interpretations and perceptions of life occur due to the pre-conscious funneling, filtering, and tunneling of neurological input over which there is no conscious control.

- Based on the limited options determined by our pre-conscious neurological mechanisms, certain thoughts, feelings, and reactions are selected to be consciously experienced. The conscious mind then takes ownership for the experiences it subsequently becomes conscious of, yet which are not consciously chosen.

- Whatever the consequences of these pre-conscious interpretations and reactions to a situation may be, these new effects further condition your neurology (outside of your conscious control), and the game continues.

When viewed from this perspective, can one honestly believe any actions taken are based on conscious will? In the end, conscious will never was—it was all an illusion. It's now time for you to discover how this illusion causes suffering and to experience the freedom found in *what is*.

Understanding Made Good

Sailors understand that a boat's velocity alone is not an accurate measure of actual progress. The wind may allow them to go very fast in a certain direction, but it may not be the direction they wish to go. Velocity Made Good (VMG) is what matters in sailing. It is the actual progress made toward a destination.

In a similar way, Understanding Made Good is what ultimately matters to the spiritual seeker. It is the actual progress made in seeing through the illusion of a separate self. Keep in mind that a genuine illusion is not just an obvious absurdity. It has aspects that are very plausible. That's why it's an illusion and why apparent progress can often be a deception for the spiritual seeker.

Thus, the true value of any spiritual teaching is measured primarily by the degree to which it liberates us from the illusion of a separate self. Realizing there is no "me" who is "doing" means "I am done" (note the double meaning!). There is only the realization that you were free all along.

Honestly investigating *what is,* at the most basic levels, is what ripens understanding for the spiritual seeker. The letting go of false premises will happen naturally as understanding deepens. *What is,* is always here waiting patiently to be discovered. No struggle is required. Your inherent spiritual curiosity is enough. Honest investigation simply aims that curiosity in the appropriate direction in order to maximize your Understanding Made Good.

A question: "What would you have to do to get out of a hole you never fell into, but thought you did?"

"Nothing," is the common response, but this misses the point. There would have to be an understanding that you never fell into a hole for you to stop trying to get out. The spiritual seeker asks the awakened how to get out of the hole of separateness and suffering. The awakened points to the fact that they never fell into a hole in the first place. "Thank you," the seeker replies, "but do you think I should use a ladder to climb out of the hole?" The awakened points again to the fact that there never was a hole and they never fell into it. "Thank you," the seeker responds, "so perhaps a rope would be better to get out of this hole?" The awakened then points again to the fact that the seeker is not in a hole.

This is what the conversation is like for one who has awakened. Yet, the awakened continues pointing with great compassion. One day the spiritual seeker understands that "the hole" was all an illusion. The seeker and the awakened can then both laugh at how simple it all is.

Investigation

As stated earlier, the broad structure of our neurology is inherited and is then fine-tuned by the experiences encountered throughout life. The tendencies inherent in our neurology often choose consistency and completeness over accuracy. Yet, for the earnest spiritual seeker it is accuracy that is of penultimate importance. It is only understanding *what is* that is required for an awakening, but precision is required for such an understanding to arise.

The investigation that follows is just another experience, but it will assist in undoing the habitual way your neurology tends to view the world. Each repetition of the investigation is like snipping a few threads on an illusionary straight jacket that has kept you in imaginary bondage. At a certain point, enough of the fabric has been snipped away and you are effortlessly released. All that remains is the actuality of what you are.

There is still no "control" over your neurology, but this investigation shifts the tendencies of interpretation that occur at the pre-conscious level. This investigation simply tosses a different orientation into the chain of cause and effect. An increased sense of well-being from Understanding Made Good is a common result.

What follows is a short series of questions. The answers are obvious for those who have read the previous chapters, and one version of an answer is even written below each question. The questions are asked to deepen your understanding and thereby re-orient your awareness. Ideally these questions will help you see through the narrow tunnels of perception that allow ignorance to persist.

Read, *genuinely consider*, and answer the following questions. Doing so in writing or out loud deepens understanding most effectively for some. For others, walking while doing the exercise is profoundly effective. Understanding through experience is the aim.

Much like plunging into a cool mountain stream, many of you will find this investigation quite refreshing. The benefits can be profound, so indulge in this inquiry as often as the desire to understand arises.

Remember, thinking one knows the answer is never the same as discovering the answer. Hopefully, you have already realized that freedom often lies in the uninvestigated details.

Exercise

This is a several-part process. Begin by identifying an event and then go through the subsequent steps to re-cognize that event. This simple exercise is a gentle way to understand *what is* and to experience the peace and freedom that comes from Understanding Made Good. The exercise requires no struggle, only your genuine spiritual curiosity.

1) Think of a situation, past or present, where negative thoughts and feelings still arise. Write it down or say it out loud. Allow

the intensity of those images and feelings to arise once again. *Experience them as much as possible.* Bring up all the judgmental "should haves" and "should be's" your mind can muster. Acknowledge consciously how the body's neurology reacts to that situation. Write all the reactions down or say them out loud. It is important to let your neurology experience fully the current perceptions about this situation, so don't hold back.

Rate the overall intensity of these feelings from 0 to 10, with 10 being the most intense.

2) Answer the following questions as best as you can. Compare this to the answers provided in italics following each question.

Is there any conscious will involved in how my neurology senses, interprets, constructs, and perceives this or any other situation?

No, my neurology does what it does. There is no conscious will.

Is there any conscious will involved in choosing the thoughts and feelings that arise within my neurology?

No, my neurology does what it does. There is no conscious will.

Is there any conscious will involved in my neurology's reaction to this situation or any other?

No, my neurology does what it does. There is no conscious will.

3) Now consider any other person(s) involved with this situation and answer the same questions.

Is there any conscious will involved in how their neurology senses, interprets, constructs, and perceives this situation?

No, a neurology does what it does. There is no conscious will.

Is there any conscious will involved in this person(s) choosing the thoughts and feelings that arise within their neurology?

No, a neurology does what it does. There is no conscious will.

Is there any conscious will involved in their neurology's reaction to this situation or any other situation?

No, a neurology does what it does. There is no conscious will.

How would it feel if I were that person(s)?

I would feel exactly the way they do because I would have their neurology that reacts exactly the way it does.

4) Now returning to the original situation, consider these questions.

Was it possible to use conscious will to control my thoughts, feelings, and reaction patterns in regard to this situation?

No, my neurology does what it does. There is no conscious will.

Was this situation any different for the other person(s) in being able to use conscious will to control their thoughts, feelings, and reaction patterns?

No, a neurology does what it does. There is no conscious will.

What is it like to experience this situation with the understanding that there is no conscious will available to my neurology or the neurology of others?

There is only the experiencing of a neurology doing what it does.
I am left as the experiencing of neurologies doing what they do in a world that is what it is.

How does this situation feel when I see through the illusion of conscious will?

I am free to experience what is, as it is, not as an illusionary conscious will wishes it was.

5) Bring up the situation again in your awareness and rate the overall intensity of feelings from 0 to 10.

What is the experiencing of this situation like now with a deeper understanding?

Has there been a shift in regard to the illusion of conscious will in this situation?

Can you feel compassion arise for your own neurology and that of others?

Repeating this investigation with this situation or other situations can be very enlightening. Notice the shift that takes place in your sense of well-being as understanding deepens.

6) Now, coming back to the larger picture, consider these final questions.

Do I understand that the wiring and firing of all neurologies is not open to conscious will?

Yes, neurologies just do what they do, i.e. people do what they do.

7) Repeat this exploration as often as the desire arises.

The point of the above exercise is for you to understand, through experience, that the story of a situation viewed through the lens of an illusionary conscious will is what creates suffering. What you have yearned for as a spiritual seeker has always been right here, right now, residing in the actuality of *what is*. These first five chapters have given you a taste of the freedom that occurs by seeing through what you are not. The final chapters will give you a taste of the joy found in discovering what you ultimately are.

Re-Orientation: I Am Awareness

Seeing through the illusion of conscious will can be very threatening. Odds are that most of your experience has been interpreted through the filter of a "me," a body and mind with conscious will, so seeing through it brings into question what you fundamentally are. The core of your previously presumed identity immediately begins dissolving, and without a "me" orienting your experience, it would appear that there is nothing left to be. The point of this chapter is to show that you are exactly the *no-thing* that remains, an unconditioned awareness of experiencing.

I Am

"I am" to the average person means, "I am a separate body and mind with conscious will that perceives through the senses." They do not see through the illusion of the separate self, so they suffer. This confusion is why so many seekers continually ask *who* they are instead of *what* they are.

Realizing the body has no conscious will drastically changes the interpretation of the statement, "I am." "I" is no longer a personal identity. "I" becomes an impersonal awareness of existing, and when "I" is impersonal, everything changes.

Spiritual seekers instinctively know that what they ultimately are is eternal. *Eternal means timeless.* All the major religions point toward this eternality. Any belief in an afterlife or other life is an intuitive attempt to understand this eternality. Your body and its neurology are not eternal. They are in time. Thus, it is not what you ultimately are.

When we grasp that all the previous perceptions of what human beings are has been a massive misinterpretation, what we are left with is each person as an eternal awareness of living and nothing more. One is then able to be their own eternality as the pure subjectivity of awareness.

Being the pure subjectivity of awareness may sound quite esoteric, but it is just the awareness of the experiencing that is happening all the time. The illusion of conscious will just blocks the conscious experiencing of it. Anyone who has been in a flotation tank can usually relate to what it is like to be pure awareness. As the body becomes weightless in the salty water and the mind relaxes into the darkness, our physical sensations of separateness are lost. When this occurs, it becomes clear that we are more an awareness of this flowing 'river of thought' than we are a thinker. One forgets the body for moments at a time, and our thoughts just float by like clouds in the sky. It is clear that thoughts rise and fall of their own accord. The awakened simply understands that this is true for all of our experiencing.

With no objective qualities of any kind, awareness is best described as a no-thing, but the tool of language has a very difficult time describing something that is no-thing. Thus, all the confusion! Truly grasping the zeroness of "I am awareness" is the critical intuition. Only then is there peace.

The Awakened: How many are here?

Seeker: I count two.

The Awakened: I count only one.

Seeker: Is this because you are one with everything?

The Awakened: No. It is because I am no-thing to be counted.

Re-Orientation

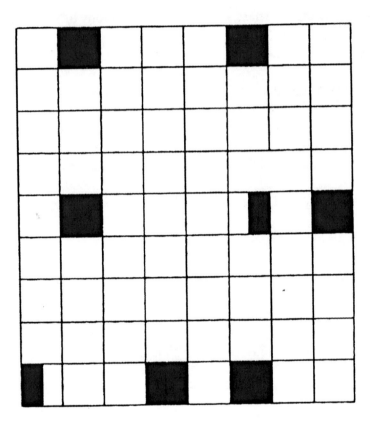

Look at the image above. What does it say? To most folks, the image looks like an empty crossword puzzle that does not seem to say anything.

Now raise the image up so it is at about eye level (higher than the tip of your nose). Tilt the page away from your eyes and look across the page. The page should be almost parallel with the floor as you look across it at eye level. There is a word spelled out that can be seen when looking across the image.

The first vertical line on the left that runs the length of the image along with the bottom left block make the letter "L." The second and third vertical lines from the left and the two blocks between them make the letter "A." The letters "U," "G," and "H" all follow in the same manner.

When looking at the above image in one way, it looked like an empty crossword puzzle. When looked at another way, the word "LAUGH" clearly appears.

Like the image above, the realization of "what" you are requires only a different way of looking. It's a reorientation that allows for a simple recognition of what has been there all along, but from a perspective that most are unable to discover. Looked at one way, you are a separate being with conscious will, a "me." Looked at another way, you are the pure subjectivity of awareness. As the unawakened, you are the "me-ing." As the awakened, you are the be-ing (as a verb).

Ambiguity

The image above is called an ambigram. Regardless of whether it is right side up or upside down, it appears the same. However, being right side up or upside down is very important for everything else on the page. Your mistaken identity as a separate "me" leaves everything else in life upside down, and this is the cause of your suffering.

The tragedy of the spiritual seeker lies in their ambiguity. Zero ambiguity in regard to an illusionary separate individual living life with conscious will is all that is required to awaken. Zero ambiguity regarding the illusion leaves everything else in life right side up. Through a simple re-orientation, you move through the world experiencing *what is*.

Orientation

makes all the difference!

Shifting orientation is the master key that the spiritual seeker has been looking for. The shift effectively occurs through understanding *what is*. However, there is an ancient exercise where one imagines "having no head" that can give you a temporary glimpse of what this orientation is like. Take a moment and give it a try.

> Imagine the thing above your shoulders we call a "head" has been removed. In its place imagine only "the pure awareness of being." "I am awareness" is all that is left where your head used to be. It helps the experiencing if your eyes are opened extra wide.
>
> Notice there is only the awareness of a body and all that surrounds it. Having no head leaves "I am awareness" as the experiencing of everything encountering that point of awareness that sits on top of your shoulders.
> There is only the experiencing of impersonal awareness as it is being lived. There is no illusionary conscious will to be found.[14]

Driving while "having no head" can also be fun. As you drive, imagine that instead of moving through the world, the world

is moving through you. In this case the you is "I am awareness."
As "I am awareness," you become the focal center for all of your
experiencing. It may take a bit of playing to make the shift, but
when the shift occurs, your experiencing changes, and with it
comes a temporary letting go of the false notion of a "me" with
conscious will moving through the world. This exercise gives a
wonderful glimpse into the world without the illusion of "me,"
yet only with understanding is the "me" seen through and forever
changed.

Take a moment and imagine a person in the middle of
paradise standing behind one simple row of prison bars. See this
person gripping the bars with both hands and pressing his or her
head between them. There is only one row of bars, so this is not
a cage, but it surely seems like one from the perspective of the
person railing against them.

The one who struggles is imprisoned only by a lack of
understanding. Freeing this person from the illusion of being
imprisoned requires only an honest inquiry into the actuality of
the situation. All it takes is a simple re-orientation. Awakening to
enlightenment is no different. It is only a different way of looking

that allows one to see through the illusion of conscious will. It is only this illusion that keeps us believing we are imprisoned in separateness. As we will see in the next chapter, only with this re-oriention can re-integration occur. Only then can you (as awareness) embrace *this-here-now* as what you phenomenally are.

From Here to Here

Re-Integration: Awakening to Enlightenment

There is a scene in the movie, *The Bear,* where a little bear cub is about to be attacked by a mountain lion. The little cub stands on its hind legs in an attempt to look intimidating. He is very impressed with himself when the mountain lion turns and runs away. What the little cub does not see is his 10-foot tall, 1200-pound father standing upright behind him. The illusionary "me" with conscious will is very much like the bear cub. They both ignore the massive weight that other causes and effects play in how any situation turns out. The "me," like the cub, is pleased when things turn out as desired, but suffers when they do not because of an inability to see *what is.*

Most individuals ignore any clues that the "me" might be deluding itself, so their experiencing of life continues as a "me." As a spiritual seeker, there is a natural curiosity that something else might be going on. Yet, for most spiritual seekers, letting go of their somebodyness is a bit like the following joke:

> Lawyer: I'm suing you for malpractice on behalf of John Smith.
>
> Psychiatrist: But why? He was completely cured by my treatment.
>
> Lawyer: My client says before your treatment he thought he was Jesus Christ. Now he feels like a nobody.

This-Here-Now

The awakened understands that the no-thingness of awareness, a pure subjectivity, a perfectly unconditioned receptivity, cannot experience itself—after all, it is not a thing. The pure subjectivity of awareness requires the phenomenal world as its complement for the dance of experiencing to occur. One without the other would make experiencing any thing impossible. The awakened understands and celebrates that what they are is the experiencing itself.

As the no-thingnesss of awareness, devoid of any phenomenal qualities, what you are can only be experienced phenomenally as *this-here-now*. Your re-integration back into the phenomenal world automatically occurs when experiencing *this-here-now*. As you re-orient into the no-thingness of awareness, you are re-integrated as the everythingness of experiencing *this-here-now.*

What you are is not just the awareness of all your conscious experiencings (i.e. thoughts, feelings, emotions, images, memories, sensations, etc.). Ultimately what you are is the awareness as the entire experiencing of *this-here-now.* I am awareness experiencing myself as everything in my awareness.

As awareness, I am realized to be no-thing, zero, zip, nadda, neti-neti, which leads to the experiencing of *this-here-now* as what "I am." In an odd way, there is no one to become enlightened! There is only the nothingness of awareness and the everythingness of experiencing *this-here-now.* Accepting your "zeroness" is where suffering ends, because there is no-thing to suffer. Embracing your everythingness as the experiencing of *this-here-now* is where celebration eternally begins.

The eternal "I" is not a phenomenal self; it is your continual, eternal phenomenal experiencing. As the nothingness of awareness, a pure subjectivity, you appear as whatever you are.

As complicated as this may seem at times, rest assured, this is not a complicated understanding. One morning while showering, I recalled how the Sufi mystic Rumi had summed it up in just three words. I took out my shower crayon (yes, I use crayons) and wrote on the shower door,

Seeing, Seeing, Seeing...

Rumi

When I returned that evening, I found my girlfriend had jokingly written beneath the Rumi quote:

Beeing, beeing, beeing...

The Hive

"Fantastico!" I thought (I had just returned from Italy); the bees are "being lived" as bees. The bees are "being beed" as part of the greater hive. So too, our bodies are "being lived" in an even greater hive. Bees do not have enough consciousness to have an illusion of separateness, so there is no suffering. They are not aware of being aware and thus have a dissociated sense of awareness. The average person has a differentiated sense of awareness and suffers. They are aware that they are aware, but they have an illusion of separateness. The awakened has an integrated sense of awareness and no longer suffers. They are aware that they are aware, but have seen through the illusion of separateness.

As the eternal "I am," there is only freedom. The "I am"

is not freed when awakening happens because it was never bound. There is only an awakening to the understanding that as awareness, "the experiencing of *this-here-now* is what I am," which has always been free.

Separateness between self and others has disappeared for the awakened. In a sense, there are no others. As awareness, there is no separation, and thus, no desperation. They are not a separate entity in an ocean desperately resisting the currents and tide. They are the continual experiencing in an ocean called *this-here-now*. They are no longer a separate perceiver, but are the perceiving.

Years ago I was reading a new book devoted to the Buddhist concept of "one taste." I put the book down and went to run an errand. Oddly, upon my return the book was missing. However, there were two little black and white puppy butts sticking out from under the couch. I knew what this meant. I peered under the couch and saw two adorably tenacious terrier puppies fully engrossed in destroying my book. Anger arose, but quickly passed as I laughed at my puppies literally taking a taste of "one taste."

I was reminded of the monk whose satori experience involved the ringing of a temple bell. He said, "There was no bell, and no me. There was only the ringing." So too, with my precious book. There was no book and no puppies chewing it. There was only the joyful tasting of the entire experience.

The awakened recognizes that this-which-in-eternity-we-are is always this, always here, always now. Enlightenment is what we are.

> A King and a sage died at the same time and ended up facing God together.
>
> "When you said, 'I am God,' it angered me," God said to the King. "I cannot allow you the highest place in the afterlife."
>
> "When you said, 'I am God,' I felt loved," God said to the sage. "I'm granting you the highest place in the afterlife."
>
> "Why are you treating us differently if we both said the same thing?" asked the King.
>
> "When you said 'I am God,' you were talking about you," sighed God. "When the sage said, 'I am God,' he was talking about me."

The King and the sage in the above story have one major difference. The King believes himself to be a separate, independent entity with conscious will. The sage has seen through the illusion of conscious will and the illusionary separateness it brings. The sage has re-oriented as the no-thingness of awareness and as a result is re-integrated as the experiencing of *this-here-now*, continually.

Only More So

The world after awakening to enlightenment is exactly as your world is right now, only more so. With no illusion of separateness, the awakened is now the *entire* experiencing of whatever is. Awakening to the actuality of *what is* makes everything exactly as it is, only more so.

For the awakened, everything is different and everything is exactly the same. Tastes in music, art, food, humor, etc. remain essentially the same. Thoughts and feelings continue to arise of their own accord just as before. Family and friends remain as they are. The history of every body is absolutely the same, down to the smallest detail. If there is a memory of dropping an ice cream cone at age five, that memory remains. The only difference for the awakened is that they are no longer distracted by the illusion of separateness. This leaves everything exactly as it has always been, only more so.

The awakened rests in the understanding that there is no

conscious choice over the perceptions, thoughts, and feelings that arise within us. There is understanding that each human being is a unique pattern of neurological development and adaptation that functions outside any concept of conscious will. Each neurology simply encounters life situations and reacts in its own idiosyncratic way. The already established neurology just does what it does. After all, how could it not?

Being linked in the chain of cause and effect does not confuse the awakened. There is no struggle and strain as the chain unwinds. Everyone and everything still does what they do within the chain. There is an understanding that no one in the physical world acts as pure causality. When investigated, our experiencing is understood to be a long chain of linked effects, each prior effect becoming the cause for another effect as the chain unwinds. This understanding allows the awakened to effortlessly be the experiencing of life itself.

Enlightenment

Awakening to enlightenment occurs directly through freedom from separate selfhood. "Freedom from separate selfhood" means that what is considered as self is not separate in any way from any thing else. Any illusionary separate self would be understood as a case of mistaken identity.

Humanity's case of mistaken identity lies at the core of its suffering. It leaves you as an illusionary separate object. Separate objects suffer. Period. "Freedom from separate selfhood" not only ends suffering, but leads to a natural living of the Golden Rule, which promotes treating others as you would like to be treated. It arises naturally out of the non-separateness that occurs as the experiencing of *this-here-now* as what I am.

A natural shift occurs when what "I am" is no longer considered the "me." Before the shift, the "me with conscious will" trembles at walking the high-tension wire of life all alone. Naturally, there is great fear of the separate "me" falling to its death. The re-orientation to being awareness allows fear to disappear. Walking the high-tension wire occurs without the gravity of the illusionary "me." Re-integration brings with it the joy of the entire high-wire act as the experiencing of what you are. The view is breathtaking. The crowd is spectacular. The body is amazing in its own right. The same experience is entirely different. Realizing that what you are is the experiencing of life adds the joyful seasoning to awareness we have come to call "enlightenment."

Enlightenment is merely an awakening to the unambiguous understanding of *what is*. That's all it is. It is seeing through the illusion of the way this world seems to operate. It does not mean that a body organism, an "earth suit," becomes perfect. There are no sudden psychic powers attained by a body upon awakening to enlightenment. One is not suddenly able to transcend the laws of physics and perform miracles. There is simply an awakening to the continual miracle of the experiencing that is happening right here, right now. *The spiritual seeker yearns for something extraordinary, but what is extraordinary is seeing the ordinary as extraordinary and the extraordinary as ordinary.*

Seeing through the illusion of the "me" as an independent entity with conscious will is all that is required for this awakening to enlightenment. Once there is a full realization of your no-thingness, the only thing left to be is the everythingness of experiencing. The body then continues to live in this world as part of the experiencing of *this-here-now*. Thus, the saying, "Before enlightenment, chop wood and carry water. After enlightenment, chop wood and carry water."

The body and its neurology will continue to do what it does. It still functions in the world because it is part of the world.

There was an awakened Master who, as a spiritual teacher, was continually pointing out to his students that the world, as they knew it, was illusion. One day a messenger arrived during a lecture and announced the death of the Master's son. Naturally, the Master began to weep.

Upon seeing the Master weeping, one student raised his hand and said, "Master, you lecture day after day that this world, as we know it, is illusion. Yet, upon hearing of the death of your son, you weep?"

"Yes," said the Master, "And there is no greater illusion than having your son die."

Upon awakening to enlightenment, there is still joy and sadness, pain and pleasure, love and compassion. The experiencing of life does not stop. The experiencing is simply not resisted by an illusionary "me." As awareness, "I am" the experiencing of *this-here-now* as what "I am," continually. That's all it is!

Who Gets Enlightened?

Many masters have uttered, "You are already enlightened." Confusion results if there is not a distinction drawn between the "me" and what you are as awareness. When it is said that "you" are already enlightened, they are not talking about a "me" that interprets the world in a manner that is personal. They are not talking about the illusionary "me" with its false concept of conscious will. As a matter of fact, they are talking about anything but that small illusionary "me" which prevents the seeing of *what is*.

It would be more accurate to say, "The ever-present 'I am,' as the continual experiencing of *this-here-now,* is already enlightened." This leaves awakening to enlightenment as simply a re-orientation to that which you already are. The illusionary "me," as an entity with conscious will, can never reach enlightenment. No separate self gets to be enlightened. That is the cosmic joke!

When the spiritual seeker finally understands *what is*, the formula is much like this:

"I Am"

Zeroness (awareness)

Experiencing

Twoness (duality, separateness)

as Oneness (*this-here-now*).

As we will see in the next chapter, in realizing the zero-ness of awareness we pass through the "gateless gate," the illusionary problem disappears, and our journey is complete.

From Here to Here

In, *Through the Looking Glass,* the Red Queen has the landscape move along with her as she runs, so no progress is ever made. The Red Queen is the perfect analogy for spiritual seekers, who must understand that none of us ever progress beyond the landscape of *this-here-now.* There is nowhere else to look. Enlightenment is always here, right now. It is what we *always* are. Enlightenment is only the realization of *what already is.*

The spiritual seeker's progress begins when they stop running and understand that they need only see the current landscape for what it is. To awaken, they only need to see through their illusion of separateness.

Enlightenment is simply an awakening to "things as they are." The landscape does not change; what changes is the way it is seen when free of the illusion of conscious will.

The Illusory Problem

His most clever student presented the awakened with an "unsolvable" problem.

> "If a small gosling is kept in a large glass bottle and fed until it is full grown," said the student, "how does one get the goose out of the bottle without breaking the bottle or killing the goose?"

> The awakened paused for a moment as everyone in the room contemplated this perplexing problem. He then tossed his small cup of water into the student's face and shouted, "Wake up!"

> As the student sat in open-mouthed shock, the awakened gently smiled and said, "The goose is out!"

The goose in the bottle was only an imaginary problem. It existed only in the mind. The only problem of the spiritual seeker is his or her inability to see through the illusion of an imaginary separate self. The separate self is only in your mind. It's not really there. The goose is already out!

This is why awakening to enlightenment is referred to as "the gateless gate." This is why a letting go of what never existed requires no effort, only understanding. In actuality, there is no "me" to become extinct. There is only the falling away of an illusionary "me" that never even existed. How much simpler could it be?

Spiritual awakening is a simple process, but also a subtle one. Most spiritual seekers are like a man who faces west each morning with the hope of witnessing a sunrise. His orientation makes seeing a sunrise impossible. Until he understands that what is being sought lies in the other direction, there will only be frustration.

The typical spiritual seeker desires the joy of being nonseparate awareness, but also wishes to maintain an identity as a separate individual with conscious will. This is like vigorously rowing a boat that is still tied to the dock. All the "rowing" is for naught if there is a lack of basic understanding. With understanding, the illusion of conscious will is untied, and awareness as the experiencing of *this-here-now* does all the work.

Your case of mistaken identity as a separate entity with conscious will is an inherent part of the human experience. The illusion of conscious will is just part of the game. Like a child pretending they are Superman, it's all good fun. No one is hurt when they tie a cape around their neck. It's when they jump off the roof that the suffering begins. It is moving through life believing in the illusion of conscious will that results in human suffering.

If enlightenment were any thing, it would be a wonderful beast that swallows whole your illusion of separateness. Thus, the saying of the Buddhist monks, "If you see the Buddha on the road, kill him." "Kill" means to see through the illusion of separateness, regardless of what that illusion is. It is only the illusion of separateness that prevents an awakening to enlightenment.

The Journey Complete

The journey from here to here is complete when there is an understanding that with no conscious will, we are left as the awareness of living. As awareness, I am the experiencing of *this-here-now* as what I am, continually. This is enlightenment.

Enlightenment is what we are. Each and every time this understanding deepens, a little more of your false identity relaxes itself away. Seeing through what is false is all that is required.

When your mistaken identity has been pulled out from under you, like a chair taken away in the game of musical chairs, there is no hard crash to the floor; there is only the blissful fall into enlightenment.

So, let's break it down one last time:

Conscious will makes non-sense when actually investigated. There is no conscious choice in the wirings and workings of your neurology. There is no conscious choice in what you think, what you feel, and ultimately what experiencing occurs in your life. In the end, the perceptions and reactions to life's infinite situations are neurologically based and pre-consciously determined. They are not consciously willed.

Belief in a body with conscious will, labeled the "me," is the lynchpin of separateness and suffering. However, the "me" has been exposed for what it is and is now like a magician who continues doing tricks in front of an audience that knows how they are performed. It's never the same once you understand the illusion.

Understanding there is no conscious will leads directly to the ultimate understanding of the "I" as "I am awareness." As awareness, I am a pure subjectivity, an absolute receptivity, a no-thingness with no objective or phenomenal qualities at all. As awareness, "I am" the experiencing of *this-here-now*, continually. As the experiencing of *this-here-now*, which is all I can ever be, I am always already enlightened.

Absorbed in the magnificence of experiencing *this-here-now*, you are at peace without reason. Understanding has erased any illusion of separateness and you are left as pure experiencing.

The journey from here to here is complete. All that remains is a celebration:

I am this!

I am here!

I am now!

That's all it is!

Are you laughing?

Afterword

Upon reflection, there are two questions that occasionally arise for readers who have completed *From Here to Here: Turning Toward Enlightenment*. The two questions and responses are as follows:

Can people change?

Yes, people can change. *However, neither the desire to seek change, nor the change itself, is consciously willed.* People's reactions to situations, on all levels, are based on their genetics and conditioning.

People can and do change with new conditioning, but mere exposure to new conditioning is not necessarily enough to manifest change. The new conditioning must be uniquely appropriate in its type, timing, and strength to override already established conditioning.

Most people can relate to having a long-sought change

occur when these three factors "finally" came together. The reason the change did not occur sooner is because these factors cannot be consciously willed into being. If personal change were under the conscious control of people (a.k.a. neurologies), then the world would be a very, very different place.

Also, the more firmly established a neurological pattern is, the more difficult it is to change. For instance, personality traits are relatively fixed by genetics and early conditioning. Thus, it generally takes very strong conditioning to change them.

Neurologies simply do what they do without consciously choosing their reactions to the situations they encounter. Recognizing that change cannot be consciously willed results in a natural flowing of compassion towards those that are suffering. How could compassion not flow when there is true understanding?

This understanding is critical for the spiritual seeker because if changes in neurological reaction patterns are assumed to be consciously willed, then captivity within humanity's primary illusion will not end. It doesn't matter if the changes in neurological patterns are large or small; they are still outside conscious control.

Seeing through the entire illusion of separate selves with conscious wills is what makes way for residing in what you always already are, the experiencing of this-here-now, continually—a miracle.

What is the point of life if there is no conscious will?

The point is that you are the miracle of experiencing each moment. You are the continual, miraculous *experiencing* of this-here-now. A separate, illusionary *experiencer* continually misses the miracle precisely because their perception is based on a misinterpretation, the illusion of conscious will.

You have spent your entire lifetime thinking that you were steering your neurology down the road of life. Now, you recognize that there is only a child's plastic steering wheel in your hands. The illusion of control is gone, but in its place is the freedom to be the breathtaking experiencing of each moment. The road still twists and turns because that is what roads do, but now the experiencing itself is what you are.

Lastly, the question "What's the point?" can only be asked from the perspective of a now infamous illusionary self with conscious will. The question itself may best be viewed as a futile attempt at "false-self preservation," the parting gesture of an illusion with only a memory of its former prominence, the sigh of resignation from a con man whose ruse has finally been exposed for all to see. Perhaps a gentle and fond wave goodbye is in order, for things will never be quite the same.

Endnotes:

[1] Wei Wu Wei, *All Else Is Bondage* (Fairfield, Iowa: Sunstar Publishing Ltd.,1999), p. 13.

[2] Coleman Barks *The Essential Rumi* (New York: Harper Collins Publishing, 1995), p. 281.

[3] Francis Crick, *The Astonishing Hypothesis* (New York: Touchstone, 1995), p. 81.

[4] Howard Bloom, *Global Brain*, (New York: John Wiley and Sons, Inc. 2000)

[5] *Ibid*, p.69.

[6] "funneling" and "tunneled" is the author's terminology.

[7] Matt Ridley, *The Red Queen* (New York: HarperCollins Publishers, Inc. 2003), p. 175.

[8] Voltaire, *Candide* (New York: Penguin Books, 1947), p. 96.

[9] Yuichi Shoda, Walter Mischel, Phillip Peake, Predicting Adolescent Cognitive and Self-regulatory Competencies From Preschool Delay of Gratification, *Cognitive Psychology*, 26, 6, (1990) pp.978-86.

[10] Robert Cialdini, Ph.D., *Influence* (New York: Quill, 2000), pp.211.

[11] Ibid, p.290.

[12] Zimbardo, P.Z, The Stanford Prison Experiment, (n.d.). Retrieved July 18, 2005 from http://www.prisonexp.org.

[13] Francis Crick, *The Astonishing Hypothesis* (New York: Touchstone, 1995), p. 3.

[14] Douglas E. Harding, On Having No Head (Carlsbad: Inner Directions Publishing, 2002)

Printed in the United States
123339LV00002B/63/A